DANCES FOR
FLUTE & THUNDER

DANCES FOR
FLUTE & THUNDER

PRAISES, PRAYERS, AND INSULTS

POEMS FROM THE ANCIENT GREEK

TRANSLATED BY BROOKS HAXTON

VIKING

The author would like to thank his family, friends and the editors of the following magazines where some of these poems appeared: *The Atlantic Monthly, Bomb, Ohio Review, Third Bed,* and *Poetry Magazine.*

VIKING
Published by the Penguin Group
Penguin Putnam Inc., 375 Hudson Street,
New York, New York 10014, U.S.A.
Penguin Books Ltd, 27 Wrights Lane,
London W8 5TZ, England
Penguin Books Australia Ltd, Ringwood, Victoria, Australia
Penguin Books Canada Ltd, 10 Alcorn Avenue,
Toronto, Ontario, Canada M4V 3B2
Penguin Books (N.Z.) Ltd, 182–190 Wairau Road,
Auckland 10, New Zealand

Penguin Books Ltd, Registered Offices:
Harmondsworth, Middlesex, England

First published in 1999 by Viking Penguin,
a member of Penguin Putnam Inc.

10 9 8 7 6 5 4 3 2 1

LIBRARY OF CONGRESS CATALOGING-IN-PUBLICATION DATA
Dances for flute and thunder : from the ancient Greek /
translated by Brooks Haxton.
       p.   cm.
ISBN 0-670-88728-5
1. Greek poetry—Translations into English.   2. Greece—
Poetry.   I. Haxton, Brooks, 1950–
PA3622.H39D36   1999   99-19804
881'.0108—dc21

This book is printed on acid-free paper. ∞

Printed in Reynosa, Mexico
Set in Centaur
Designed by Betty Lew

Preface

A little more than twenty-five hundred years ago, on the western coast of Anatolia and on the islands nearby, poetry reached almost everyone. It was performed by soldiers, prostitutes, progressive statesmen, slaves, maiden votaries, and philosophers. They celebrated keenness of perception, thought, and feeling.

In Greek sculpture, meanwhile, the stiff smooth limbs of the Egyptian kouroi thawed, bending and rippling with the muscle of athletes and warriors. The rigid korai became young women more lifelike than ever anywhere on earth. Greek poets were bringing the psyche to life in words, just as sculptors were in stone.

Their poems still offer, much as ever, human contact, beauty, and wisdom. Yet they go unread. Other poetries from long ago, the Rig Veda, the Psalms, the Shih Ching, sustain their audience because of religious traditions while Greek lyrics and epigrams find fewer and fewer readers even in universities. Yet coming back to these poems now and taking them to heart has shaken me, for one, at the tip of a forgotten taproot. I cannot imagine anything more invigorating.

Like short poems earlier in other languages, some of the poems translated here must have been sung by their authors, or by dancing choruses, to the accompaniment of double-reeded flute, or strings. But even ordinary speech, shaped as it was in ancient Greek by purposeful variations in pitch, must have had the singing elocution we hear now, for example, in Chinese.

For a poet taking up the new technology of the Greek alphabet, with its miraculous precision, to write was to make a sound recording. To read always meant to read aloud. Though less melodic poems may not have been sung, the spoken rhythms of elegy and iamb still suggest song lyrics to an audience familiar with ballads and the blues.

For what was sung, the music is almost entirely lost. Despite much brilliant scholarship about Greek speech, no true reproduction of any ancient dialect is possible. Sung or not, danced or not, spoken aloud or not, the poetry survives, a few thousand poems at any rate, many incomplete.

Never having studied ancient Greek, I began to look at my favorite lyrics and epigrams in the original language. I wanted to get closer to poems I had found in various translations livelier, more deeply intelligent, funnier, more beautiful, and more and more moving over the years.

For every word, at first, I used Liddell and Scott's *Greek-English Lexicon*, for inflections, consulting the charts in Hansen and Quinn's *Greek: An Intensive Course*. With the help of Allen's *Vox Graeca*, I read aloud. In free translation, then, with no hope of reproducing the original prosody, I tried to deliver as much as possible of the old poems into English. More often than not, my versions maintain literal accuracy. But the freest of them are far from paraphrase.

Words, phrases, lines at a stretch are left out, or shifted in position, where the more literal version went slack. Where poems have been excerpted, condensed, combined, rearranged, and otherwise emended here, I did not work to improve the originals, but only to make my rendition as effective as possible. What I did to bring the poem alive in English serves poetry, I hope, if not scholarship. In all such judgments, I considered loss of intensity, in my version of an effective poem, a crucial loss of accuracy.

Where I could, I have specified meanings and contexts in lore that few readers could experience with the spontaneous recognition expected of the original audience. Figures of speech, and other incidental touches, anachronisms sometimes, are added for stylistic and dramatic effect. Some sensory details are specified, some heightened. In some poems, I have altered the pitch of rhetoric where my paraphrase lacked dramatic pungency.

For anyone who wants a more literal version, I recommend the books in the Loeb Classical Library, which give the Greek with prose translations into English by such scholars as W. R. Paton, J. M. Edmonds, D. A. Campbell, and D. L. Page. Another excellent book, including Greek and English, is the selection made by J. W. Mackail at the beginning of the twentieth century. Constantine A. Trypanis translated a more recent selection.

Willis Barnstone's lively versions of about half the poems in this book, and of hundreds not included here, were all I knew of the originals for some years. I hope my work, like Barnstone's and the others', will help draw readers toward the original language.

Among English versions I have read, many translators have been poets. Twentieth-century English versions of Greek poems I have found especially eye opening include those by Dudley Fitts, Mary Barnhard, Richmond Lattimore, Kenneth Rexroth, and Guy Davenport. To these writers, living and dead, thanks and respect.

Most of all, to the poets whose voices do not die, because they made what they say sing, thanks again, and always.

CONTENTS

FOR HARRIS McCARTER AND GEORGE TATGE

This water's meant for careful wading,
but imagining my ears are gills, I still dive there at night.

—Jim Harrison

SINGER

Archilochos, 7th century b.c.e.

She took the myrtle branch and sang in turn
another song of pleasure, in her left hand still
the flower of the rose tree, and let loose
over her naked shoulder, down her arm
and back, the darkness of her hair.

LIAR

Archilochos

Swept overboard, unconscious in the breakers,
strangled with seaweed, may you wake up in a gelid
surf, your teeth, already cracked into the shingle,
now set rattling by the wind, while facedown,
helpless as a poisoned cur, on all fours you puke
brine reeking of dead fish. May those you meet,
barbarians as ugly as their souls are hateful,
treat you to the moldy wooden bread of slaves.
And may you, with your split teeth sunk in that,
smile, then, the way you did when speaking as my friend.

THREE NOTES FROM THE FIELD

ARCHILOCHOS

One of them by now is gloating, holding in his hands my shield,
    a target of thick bull's hide overlaid with bronze.
I dropped it in the woods to run. Who needs this now, I said.
      Tomorrow, I can get me one no worse.

I want to fight you, soldier, as a thirsty man wants water.

When we, a thousand, overtook the seven men who ran,
    we swarmed for blood, even onto their corpses.

STRING AND REED

Archilochos

I can lead off in a song to the bittersweet Lesbian flute,
or sing Ayie to Dionysus, thunderstruck with wine.

FROM PAPYRI OXYRHYNCUS

POSSIBLY ALKMAN, 7TH CENTURY B.C.E.

We, who come among the dead as far
as to the very Goddess, nine girls,
maidens, lovely in our dancing,
in bright loveliness of folded
woven work, with fine-sawn necklaces
of ivory, shine, brilliant
to the dead eye as forgotten daylight.

SLEEP

Alkman

Peak, and chasm also, sleep, the cliff too,
where the torrent cuts and falls into the surf,
and everything bred out of the dark ground,
lizards on the warm rock faces, bees,
and monstrous creatures in the gloom under the sea,
even in flight the great-winged birds of omen, sleep.

EROS

SAPPHO, 7TH CENTURY B.C.E.

Eros, shaking under my rib cage
like a wind flung into a mountain oak,
has left me loose again in all my limbs,
my sweet, my bitter, unimaginable beast.

DESIRE

Sappho

You came to me, when I lay aching
for your touch, to soothe
under the tender place what yearns.

INSCRIPTION ON A WINE JUG

SAPPHO

Beside the temple where stone altars
smoke with incense our small grove
of apple trees regales us.

Murmurings of a cold spring rise here
through the apple branches to a slope
where grass-blades flicker under the trance
of white rose petals and young leaves.

There, in the meadow, horses graze
among the blossoms which the winds
tip toward us, and away.

Love herself comes here, none other,
she who pours out into the golden cups
in our cupped hands the only nectar
fit for her festivities.

ADONIS AND APHRODITE

Sappho

From the wound death spreads into the delicate limbs.
    What shall we do for him, Goddess?

Cry. Rip the coarse stitch of your robe, my girls,
    and cry, and tear the fine threads underneath.

YOU WHO SPURNED ME AND MY SONG

SAPPHO

Dead, no thought of you from anyone
who wants or wishes anything,
not one word said concerning you, forgotten,
wavering beyond extinction, may you be
unseen, and restless there, among the corpses.

AEOLIAN ODE

SAPPHO, LESS OFTEN ATTRIBUTED TO ALKAIOS

In ancient Crete around Love's altar where the delicate
grasses flowered graceful women with a quickening
of soft footsteps kept time in the choral dance.

DOG DAYS

ALKAIOS, 7TH CENTURY B.C.E.

Wet those thirsty pipes, my friend, with two parts water,
one part wine, for now the Dog Star swings around again
to parch the world—the scourge of everything alive
except that ghost bloom of a thistle and the dry cicada
ringing with an iron rasp under the wilted leaves. Now
our women bleed for love, and find us wizened in the heat,
dry from the gourd with brains arattle into the creaking knees.

FRAGMENT FROM PAPYRI OXYRHYNCUS

Alkaios

All ... demolish ... burn ...
I gain control ... I suffer ...
shameful ... O! [a person's name?] ...

THE BRIDE

Erinna, 7th century b.c.e.

Of me, the bride, you at my gravestone now may say
in tears as they said then that Death was envious.
The bridegroom's father, with a torch he made to light
the way home from the wedding feast, kindled my pyre,
and those who loved me sang as a bridal song my dirge.

SONG

STESICHOROS, 6TH CENTURY B.C.E.

Forget the wars with me and sing
as if the very gods delighted
in our feast, in love, and listening.
The Phrygian flutes repeat
a tender phrase, to find us
here, where swallows babble
yet again, surprised by spring.

LAST SUN IN THE TREETOPS

IBYKOS, 6TH CENTURY B.C.E.

From her roost the water hen stretched out
her purple-green sleek neck,
the kingfisher's quick glance
shook droplets from his crown,
and I thought love would always be
that brilliant on the wing and wild.

STORM

Ibykos

Under the flowering quince trees
at the riverside, where purple
blossoms on the shoots
of wrist-thick vines shade
playful faces of young women,
longing never for a moment
leaves me. While I breathe,
it burns. A cold wind
out of the lowering northwest
quickens under the forks of lightning,
old roots twist into the same
dark earth, and still
the heart clings fast, and faster.

DAIMON

ANAKREON, 6TH CENTURY B.C.E.

Cursing her fame, she said,
"Given the outcome, Mother,
it might have been better for us,
if you had taken me out
by night, and thrown me
into the breakers under a cliff."

CONSIDER THE SOURCE

Solon, 6th century b.c.e.

Out of a cloud come squalling snow and hailstones.
    Think. Blind thunder comes out of the lightning.
Out of the city, meanwhile, great men come to nothing,
    and the people, misled, follow the rule of despots.
Shipmasters less fearful of the storm are not, for that,
    the braver. Out of thought comes courage.

TO APHRODITE, DIONYSUS, AND THE MUSES

Solon

Dear to me as works of love
    are wine and feasting,
and the arts that make the mind
    more cheerful.

THE AGES OF MAN

SOLON

After the time of childish thoughts, a child
with milk teeth fallen out, past seven years,
enjoys, and after seven more outgrows, his boyhood.
Then, in the third seven, limbs still thickening,
his face with its first down flowers and changes.
In the fourth he comes fully into the strength
of manhood, signifying excellence and virtue.
In the fifth he seeks a wife and gets him children.
In the sixth he sets his mind toward learning
all things useful, and forgoes distractions.
For the seventh and the eighth age, both, in mind
and tongue, he feels the fullness of his powers.

In the ninth age, able though he may yet be,
he weakens in his wit and speaks more softly.
If he lives out ten full ages, he knows, soon
though it may be, his fate is not an early death.

TWO BLESSINGS

MIMNERMOS, 6TH CENTURY B.C.E.

Be quick, my soul, for joy, as others later will be
so, when I, with everyone I love, am senseless earth.

May truth be spoken between you and me,
and may all we do seek justice.

IN MEMORY OF THEMISTOKLES

TIMOKREON OF RHODES, 5TH CENTURY B.C.E.

Themistokles—who kept Timokreon his former host in exile,
and who helped his fellow thieves, hurt friends, and murdered
anyone you like, for money—first was ostracized,
and then, before he killed himself in shame, set up
an inn for scum and losers, whom he served cold meat.
There, at his own table, lowlife daily cursed his name.

EPITAPH

SIMONIDES, 5TH CENTURY B.C.E.

Having eaten much, drunk much, and said much ill
  of many men, here lies Timokreon of Rhodes.

EPITAPHS AT THERMOPYLAE

SIMONIDES

Four thousand of us fought three million.
When you visit Sparta, tell them:
Here, the soldiers kept their word.

This stone speaks in honor of Megistias, whom
once the Persians crossed the river Spercheios
they put to death: a seer, having seen no doubt
his cohort would be overrun, he did not leave them.

ON THE CHARACTER OF THE ISLANDERS OF LEROS

PHOKYLIDES, 5TH CENTURY B.C.E.

Lerians, I have found, are bad. Not one worse than another,
all all bad. Except Prokles. And Prokles is a Lerian.

PRAISE AND LAMENTATION

BAKCHYLIDES, 5TH CENTURY B.C.E.

Eudemos built this altar on his farmstead,
thankful that the spirit of the west wind gave
    in answer to his prayers swift help
at the winnowing of barley from the sun-split husk.

Our sweet child, lifeless, woke
    in us the woe that none may speak.

MUSIC FOR THE KING AND MEN OF MACEDONIA

BAKCHYLIDES

Not left hanging on a peg, no longer mute,
but in my hands now, harp, with voice as golden
as a feather for the King, by my skill, stir
the young men at his feast, souls warmed
by wine cups traveling from lip to lip.
Already, love soars into them, their thoughts
borne up by wine, until they would lay low
stone battlements, and be the rulers then
of everything, their houses rich with gold
and ivory, and bound for home their ships
on fair seas, sunlit, carrying them wheat
and wealth from all the lords of Egypt.

So, the seven strings persuade young men,
who soon forget their drunken foolishness,
and yet remember singing in their hearts.

INVITATION

Bakchylides

I cannot promise at my hearth
great slabs of beef, and gold,
and deep red carpet,
but only the loving-kindness
of your host, and music,
and clay crocks of local wine.

ON BECOMING A GOD,
ADONIS REMEMBERS THE WORLD

PRAXILLA, 5TH CENTURY B.C.E.

Of all I leave, most beautiful is the sunlight.
Next come stars at nightfall, and the moon's face,
and in season, peaches, muskmelons, and pears.

GIRL IN THE DOORWAY

Praxilla

The look of candor from your childhood has made you
more beautiful the more you have grown womanly
below, but you may find now under every stone,
my dear, a scorpion, to pierce, and burn the heart.

GRACE AND VIRTUE

SOCRATES, 5TH CENTURY B.C.E.

Men who dance most beautifully for the gods
are finest also on the field of war.

THREE EPITAPHS

PLATO, 4TH CENTURY B.C.E.

You, who shone as a dawn star living, dead
now, shine as an evening star, to the dead.

Sailor, be well, on the salt waves and on earth. Only
from my stone in passing read, I lie here shipwrecked.

Here under a boatswain's stone, as there under a plowboy's,
same for us as everywhere for everyone, is Hades.

THREE LOVE NOTES

PLATO

I feel, when I kiss Agathon, how recklessly my soul
  leans forward at my lips as if to step across.

When you count the stars, my love, I want to be
the night sky, looking into you with all those eyes.

I am an apple thrown to you for love. Nod yes,
  Xanthippe. You and I, though sweet, are not to last.

I, HER LAMP, AM YOURS TO FILL AND LIGHT

KALLIMACHOS, 3RD CENTURY B.C.E.

Me, a lamp of twenty wicks made rich with oil,
in grief a mother dedicated to the Lord of Hell,
the Bull, the Keeper of Canopus, star in the bright
Keel under the southern night. Me, she kept lit
in fulfilment of a vow for her lost child. Regarding
the brilliance of my flames may visitors here say,
"Look how the Evening Star, though fallen, shines."

HERAKLEITOS OF HALIKARNASSOS

Kallimachos

Someone, Herakleitos, spoke to me about your death,
and I with fresh tears thought again how many times
the two of us would talk until the sun sank. You,
too many years ago, though sacred in my memory forever
as a guest and friend, sank also into ashes. Here,
meanwhile, your poems sing to me like nightingales,
only out of the darkness where no hand can reach.

ON THE BLESSEDNESS OF APHRODITE

THEOCRITOS, 3RD CENTURY B.C.E.

.

Although we took each other that first night
as if to lose ourselves in sidelong ecstasy
under the flares of heaven, year by year
we found ourselves more fully in this world,
our children with us laughing in one house:
whoever serves this Goddess chooses well.

LANDSCAPE WITH YOUNG MAN AND SNARES

THEOKRITOS

Whatever sleep possesses you, your body
on the leaf-strewn hillside, stakes
sunk into the ground, whatever weariness
in you needs rest, beware. Nearby, Priapus,
with his lovely rough head clothed
in yellow shoots of ivy, and Great Pan
stalk, side by side, into your hiding place.
Come, loose your body from its torpor: run!

FROM THE SEVENTH IDYLL, FIRSTLINGS

THEOKRITOS

On a pallet freshly made of crushed reed stalks,
we lay together under the tall sweet flag, and drank.

Overhead, there was a flurry in the poplar leaves,
nearby, the water shushing from a sacred cave,
and in the deep shade prattle of crickets,
and the peeper on a wild raspberry cane,
with horned larks in the briars whistling,
and a goldfinch fluting her four notes
repeatedly over the low coo of a dove.
On either side wild pears and apples
thudded, and the saplings of the wild plum
bent toward us with overload of fruit.

We broke the sealing resin on another wine jar
and poured wine, mellow as the supplicant girl
brought the Goddess of the Threshing Floor.
For her, at winnowing, I thrust my shovel
into the heap of corn to make a thrilling hiss,
while she sat almost laughing with a little sheaf
of poppies in one hand and in the other wheat.

DILDO WITH NIGHTINGALES

THEOKRITOS

Where the lane under the oaks goes crooked,
friend, an image lately carved in fig wood stands,
dried up, and soft, and soon to rot, with patches
of the bark left on, ears missing and the nose,
but with a phallus fit for the God himself.
Thereby, the holiest of waters spring forth
onto the rocks, inside a sacred copse of myrtle,
bay, and fragrant cypress. Twisted everywhere
among the limbs an ancient grapevine spreads
and blooms, and particolored notes of nightingales,
metallic, honeyed as their yellow plumage, call
and answer in a choric ritual of spring. There,

friend, pray for me. Plead with the God to ease
this yearning for the young man he made irresistible,
and I shall bring a kid in sacrifice, if he says yes.
But if Priapus tips his head back once like this,
to tell you no; then, I will make a threefold
sacrifice: a goat, a heifer, and a suckling lamb.
And I will sing so achingly, the God inside
the listening boy will hear me, and be kind.

ON THE EMPTINESS OF THE TOMB

LEONIDAS OF TARENTUM, 3RD CENTURY B.C.E.

A black squall out of the east, and murk of night,
    and waves, struck under the deathwatch of Orion.
I, the handsomest of sailors, drowned, halfway to Libya,
    tumbling into the fleshpots of the crab and conger eel.
My stone says, Here Love mourns where Beauty lies undone,
    but nobody lies or mourns there but the stone.

FABLE

LEONIDAS OF TARENTUM

A billygoat with a good beard, clambering
from among his wives over the stone wall
of a vineyard, nipped the sprays and branches
all the way to the understock, which spoke up
out of the ground, as loud as any vinestock could,
"Eat, goat! Rip my tender parts! And soon
my deep-set root will send up growth again,
and nectar, fat enough inside the grape for wine
to pour on your thick head at sacrifice."

ADVICE TO TRAVELERS

Leonidas of Tarentum

No, thirsty from the climb though you may be, not yet:
sheep trample the warm mud of the streambed here,
and just beyond that outcrop browsed by heifers,
in the shade of an old pine, you will find spilling
into a stone scooped hollow by the waterfall
a spring the shepherds drink from. That one tastes
crisp as an eddy of snowflakes on the north wind.

GARLAND

MELEAGROS, 2ND CENTURY B.C.E.

White violet, narcissus, twist
of myrtle, lily, sweet with laughter,
crocus, purple hyacinth, all
interwound with rosebuds opening
as love does thoughts of her: my crown
I placed about her temples,
where the petals dropped already
into her gold braid, loose
with balm and drooping curls.

IDEA OF BEAUTY

Meleagros

Shy, he stepped off into the cornfield. I could see
    his back muscles under the damp shirt quiver and go slack.
Turning again to face the shade, he smiled at me, not
    squinted, smiled, and finished tugging shut his fly.
Now, when the cornstalks in the night wind slide
    like fire, I see him. He steps closer in my dream.
I don't know, where he sleeps, if sleep refreshes him,
    but here it works me like hot metal over a flame.

THE POET TO THE CRICKET UNDER HIS WINDOW

Meleagros

Cricket in the night, again, instead of sleep,
instead of her touch, comes your chirp,
under the matted shadow of dried grasses
where you hide and scrape your wings. It's me,
your body's instrument keeps saying, me!
You make your lifelong whining beautiful.
Forgive me if I fall asleep. I'll find you
in the morningtime, I swear, and bring fresh
sprigs of groundsel to your hiding place.
You soothe me now. Tomorrow I will mist you
with cool springwater, after the sun gets high.

FUNERAL

MELEAGROS

Cremate me, what's left, my dear.
Pour into the ashes in my urn
a fifth of sour mash, stir well,
and bury. Let my stone say,
Love gave death a snort.

UNREASON

ANONYMOUS, OF UNCERTAIN DATE AND PLACE

Everything is laughter and unthinkable dust.
Out of nothing without reason comes what is.

LAMENT FOR ADONIS

BION, 2ND CENTURY B.C.E.

The wedding torch is out, the garland shattered
on the ground. Now, mourners tend him,
hair hacked short in grief. One weeping
unties from a lifeless foot the shoe. One
with golden basin stoops to wash his thigh.

His lover stumbles in the woods without direction,
hair unbraided, bare feet plucked by thorns.
Look how her sad singing fills the world.
The rocks are sad, the little valleys weep.
The world says nothing but in echo, dead.

LAMENT FOR BION

A PUPIL OF BION, 2ND CENTURY B.C.E.

Young parsley, mallows, and the crumpled buds
of dill unfold. They grow, and die, and live again
another year. But men, grown tall, and strong,
and wise, once dead, laid senseless in a hole,
sleep underground a sleep without an end.
There is no waking. Bion, poet though he was,
is gone under the dirt and silence. Little
tree frogs make a useless noise, and I sing:
Woe, Sicilian Muse, a song of woe . . .

THE SHEPHERD AND
THE KEEPER OF THE ARCTIC BEAR

ANTIPATER OF SIDON, 2ND CENTURY B.C.E.

When at dawn Arcturus comes up
under the Shepherd's belt,
when grapes look ready for the sickle,
and men thatch their cottages for winter,
then, the poor man, with no fleece-lined coat
or woolens for indoors, begins to shiver
and to curse the brightness of this star.

ANTIGENES AND BAKCHIOS

PHILODEMOS, 1ST CENTURY B.C.E.

Now though roses bud, and peapods thicken,
though new stalks of kale make heads, and herbs
come into season, with salt goat cheese,
and the curly delicate young leaves of lettuce,
yet we do not walk out into the fields
as we have done these few years past, my dear,
since our sweet boys, Antigenes and Bakchios,
who used to dillydally on our path, today we buried.

TWO CONQUESTS

PHILODEMOS

A voice said, No: forget her touch, and keep in mind
those nights of jealousy and tears. Be strong, the voice
reminded me, as she was strong when she said, Yes,
and crowed, and grappled you for joy between her thighs.

With tearful baby talk and pleading eyes, your hands
inside my clothes, you bite your lip, for all the world
as if, with kisses and sweet dirty names, too hot to wait,
until in bed, with only me beside you, you do nothing.

CHARITO SUGGESTS A DRINK

PHILODEMOS

Sixty, with long hair as black and breasts
as small and firm as in her youth, her skin
unwrinkled as though burnished by the hands
of gods, and still her very coolness
an enticement, now she says to a new lover
unafraid of her long-burning thirst, and his,
"I need you to forget the years. Come. Drink."

HERMES, GOD OF THIS AND THAT

PHILODEMOS

Five or nine times over in a night
the god exalted me and mine, and now
he comes one measly time from early dark
till dawn: I get it up a little, if
at all, and feel half dead. The god of thieves
pickpocketed the purse he used to fill,
leaving the useless part to me, and age,
and now he leads my soul toward hell.

SONG AND DANCE

PHILODEMOS

I was a fool, in love, in lust . . . who knows?
Flinging myself at happiness, I thought . . .
as who would not? Half crazy, drunk,
with a prayer of blundering somehow
into the sacred mystery. Now gray hair
grows more than the black, and I believe
this age may suit intelligence. We did
that other dance till dawn, and now
we turn to a glimmering in the mind.

CHARON

ZONAS, 1ST CENTURY B.C.E.

You who pull the oars, who meet the dead,
who leave them at the other bank, and glide
alone across the reedy marsh, please take
my boy's hand as he climbs into the dark hull.
Look. The sandals trip him, and you see,
he is afraid to step there barefoot.

SACRIFICE

ZONAS

A pomegranate torn to show bright seed,
a peach red under the down, a giant fig
with dark skin pursed into the navel,
grapes in a cluster purple with sweet wine,
and one walnut, split in its greenish
yellow husk, these fruits, laid here
under the stone shaft of Priapus, honor him,
the god whose fullness in the growing
stem has blest me, farm and farmer.

INVOCATION TO THE BEES

ZONAS

Fetch into your singing hive the thyme
just shriveled under an early chill,
and scratch and nibble at the poppy crumb
and at the torn place in the raisin.
Also, from the soft spot on the peach,
and from the violet, bring back
your gleanings. Build your cells of wax.
And Pan, the god of bees and keeper
of the hive, will come in turn
and dip out of a drowsy smoke his hand
at honey gathering, to take his part,
to taste, and leave a share for you.

EARTHENWARE

ZONAS

Let me drink, my sweetness,
from the clay cup, I who come forth
out of the same clay,
under the same clay soon to lie forgotten.

WISDOM

Automedon, possibly 1st century b.c.e.

A man lives in the keeping of a great, good power
if he has not fallen into debt, or married,
or had children. Even one who has been rash
and taken home a wife, may yet be blessed,
if, with substantial dowry well in hand,
he buries her at once. This is wisdom
better than philosophers have sought
among the monads dancing in the void.

HERE

MARCUS ARGENTARIUS, 1ST CENTURY C.E.

Dead forever, under your little plot,
away from living things and sunlight,
may you find transcendent timelessness.
But here your wineglass holds red wine.
Here, under your arm, the shoulders
of your wife are beautiful, alive again
with laughter. Maybe the mind somewhere
transcends the grave. Here, the great
philosophers lie in a heap of skulls.

ECHO

SATYRUS, 2ND CENTURY C.E.

Up and down the meadow where the sheep graze echo,
    fadingly as afterthoughts, the cries of quail.

IN MEMORY

AMMIANUS, 2ND CENTURY A.D.

So may the dust lie light upon Nearchos,
that, with ease, the dogs may drag him out.

TOAD

AMMIANUS

Now, at the big boys' table, courting favor,
when they cry, you dab your eyes and sob,
and when they laugh, you make that choking
noise, although you have no business laughing,
and none weeping. Friends of yours say otherwise.
They say: business is one thing you always have.

DINNER CHEZ APELLES

AMMIANUS

He set before his dinner guests a meadow, sacrificed,
as if he meant to feed, instead of neighbors, goats,
with heaps of dandelions, chicory, asparagus, rue,
leeks, green onions, mint, arugula half gone to seed,
and who knew what. I grazed at first on lupine sprouts,
but thinking that the next course might be hay, I left.

MESSAGE FROM THE COURT OF APOLLO

ANONYMOUS, 4TH CENTURY C.E.

Tell your king, the sculpted walls lie fallen
in the dust. The lord of prophecy, Apollo,
keeps no shelter here, no laurel, and no priest.
No longer does the fountain in the courtyard speak.
Even the waters left here, whispering into the sun.

THE POET DESCRIBES LOVE

MARIANUS, 5TH CENTURY C.E.

Love, I tell you, has no bow, no feathered reed
to leap or strike the heart, no pretty wings,
no torch to burn the breast. He carries in his hands
three crowns, and wears a fourth. And when he comes,
he says, The senses represent my lesser part. I am not
of this earth: I light the torch of learning in the mind,
and lead the soul up into heaven. Mine to carry are
the crowns of the four virtues, Justice, Courage, Balance,
and with the first I crown myself, the crown of Wisdom.

EPITAPH

JULIANUS AEGYPTIUS, 6TH CENTURY C.E.

As I have sung ten thousand times, though dead,
I sing again, Drink up. And never mind the stains.
Nobody wears anything for long, except this coat of dust.

AN APPEAL TO THE PIETY OF A LEARNED WOMAN, REMEMBERING THE QUEEN SEMIRAMIS WHO BUILT THE WALL OF BABLYON AND KEPT THE CITY INSIDE CONSECRATED TO THE GODDESS ISHTAR AND THE MYSTERIES OF LOVE

Paulus Silentarius, 6th century c.e.

Let's toss off these heavy cloaks, my dear, and show
the wit, with limbs unwrapped, to be wrapped only
in each other's limbs, hands free from hindrance.
Even your most delicately woven robe, to my mind,
is a tawdry brickwork: inside, gardens overflowing
temples, lovelier to me than Babylon. Your naked
breast on mine, your lips on my lips, therefore,
press, and hush, in wonder, my god-awful babbling.

RAINY SEASON

ANAKREONTEIA, DATE UNCERTAIN

Black earth drinks.
Trees drink from it.
The sea drinks rivers
and the sun the sea.
I saw an old moon
drink the sun. Still
my friends say, Fight
your thirst. And I do
what I can: I drink.

CICADA

ANAKREONTEIA, DATE UNCERTAIN

People like to think of you, cicada,
when you sing down from the treetop,
having sipped the clear dew,
happy, high, and full of music
as a king, that you speak praise
of everything you see, the farms,
the woods, and under you the farmer,
grateful that you damage nothing,
holds this prophecy in honor,
portent of the summer fruit.
Even the Muses love your voice,
vibrating, as if out of the sun itself.

And old age never comes to you,
but only the earthborn wisdom
of your song, no hint of suffering,
or of the blood of passion, spirit,
we say, almost equal to the gods'.

NOTES

Singer, Archilochos: At certain drinking parties, called symposia, each person in turn would hold a myrtle branch emblematic of love and art. Before passing the branch to the next, each sang a song. Professional entertainers would have been the only women present. Many of these were prostitutes, accomplished as musicians, dancers, and poets.

Three Notes from the Field, Archilochos: Archilochos was a soldier who wrote a number of poems about warfare, largely, it seems, for an audience of soldiers. The first of these three poems, according to legend, got him expelled from the court in Sparta. He died in battle.

Liar, Archilochos: Attribution of this poem, from a fragment written on papyrus hundreds of years after Archilochos' death, is doubtful. Hipponax, another poet renowned for invective, has also been credited. Some speculate that Archilochos may have had in mind here his prospective father-in-law, Lykambes, who canceled his daughter's engagement to Archilochos, they sometimes say, because the poet's mother was a slave. The order of sentences has been shifted in this translation.

Eros, Sappho: The rationale for combining two fragments in this translation is artistic, not scholarly. This is the first recorded instance of the word *bittersweet* in Greek.

Adonis and Aphrodite, Sappho: The goddess in the original commands her followers to tear their clothes and beat their breasts. Because breast beating suggests insincerity and excessiveness in English, the contrast between coarse and fine threads is introduced to suggest a genuine sense of damage.

You Who Spurned Me and My Song, Sappho: The translation substitutes the modern horror of extinction for the Greek horror of Hades, a place-name that may strike readers of English as merely fanciful. "Hades" makes more sense in English when context emphasizes what that concept represents, as in Plato's couplet below.

Dog Days, Alkaios: The sound of the cicada is musical in the original poem. Fidelity to this point works better when the cicada is a particular focus of the poem, as in the anonymous poem at the end of this collection.

Fragment from Papyri Oxyrhyncus, Alkaios: This is the only fragment left unmended here in English. About half these translations from earlier than the fourth century B.C.E. present fragments as if they are whole poems.

Consider the Source, Solon: I doubt that this translation gets what Solon meant, but I suspect that the original made a more definitive statement than literal paraphrase suggests.

In Memory of Themistokles, Timokreon of Rhodes: Themistokles is celebrated by the historian Thucydides as a great leader of Athens and a hero in the war against the Persian invaders, praised, in particular, for his development of the city's navy, and for his tactics in the naval victories of Artemisium and Salamis. Many reports, including Herodotus, without contesting the military record, confirm Timokreon's low opinion of the man.

Epitaph, Simonides: As readers may infer from this and the next two poems, Simonides was a personal friend of Themistokles and of Megistias, and an enemy of Timokreon, who was known as a winner of the pentathlon, a supporter of the Persians in Rhodes, a glutton, and a lush. At Thermopylae, a small Greek force, vastly outnumbered, resisted the Persian army in a narrow pass.

On Becoming a God, Adonis Remembers the World, Praxilla: These lines were remembered as the occasion for a saying: "Silly as Praxilla's Adonis." To compare heavenly bodies with muskmelons was thought, in the Greek sense, hysterical. Men who dismissed Praxilla may not have understood the cult of Adonis with its emphasis on the renewed fertility of the earth, since this form of worship appealed mainly to women. In any case, scorn for these lines seems to represent a masculine, Apollonian ideal. The word in question is usually taken to mean cucumbers, rather than muskmelons. I like the poem very much either way, but, as one who grows and eats cucumbers, I find it difficult to understand the phrase "ripe cucumbers," or "cucumbers in season."

Girl in the Doorway, Praxilla: This is a combination of two fragments.

I, Her Lamp, Am Yours to Fill and Light, Kallimachos: The original poem refers to the god of Canopus, a brilliant star in the southern constellation Argos, the Ship. Egyptian theology of the underworld is introduced in this translation, because Canopus the steersman of Menelaus died when shipwrecked in Egypt. Kallimachos spent most of his own life in Egypt, where he worked as a scholar at the library of Alexandria.

On the Blessedness of Aphrodite, Theokritos: This translation contains no genuine paraphrase. The original, with its blend of sexually charged wit and piety, alludes to the worship of Aphrodite Urania versus that of Aphrodite Pandemos. Setting aside lore known to everyone in the poet's time and to no one now, I represent the dramatic core of this poem as I understand it.

Idea of Beauty, Meleagros: The anachronistic handling of "zipper" in this poem is one of many liberties taken by the translator in this and the next two poems.

Lament for Adonis, Bion: Laments for Adonis, who was called by various names in various times and places, had been sung by women in his cult for more than two thousand years when Bion wrote this literary pastiche of the tradition. This excerpt is less than a tenth of the original poem.

Lament for Bion, a pupil of Bion: This excerpt is about one tenth of the original poem.

Hermes, God of This and That, Philodemos: The Greek poem, which addresses Aphrodite, not Hermes, makes witty reference in passing to a thief, Termerus, renowned for butting his victims to death with his head. Since the wit of the double entendre did not survive my efforts to explain it, the translation uses Hermes, god of erections, thieves, and so forth, for analogous humor.

An Appeal to the Piety of a Learned Woman, Remembering the Queen Semiramis Who Built the Wall of Babylon and Kept the City Inside Consecrated to the Goddess Ishtar and the Mysteries of Love, Paulus Silentarius: The title for this poem was an effort to avoid conspicuous explanation in a text that used the adjective *Semiramidian*. The idea of a note like this one seemed pedantic.